FANCY RATS

The Fancy Rat: A Comprehensive Guide to Understanding, Caring for, and Companioning with Your Pet Rat

The behavior, health, housing, diet, training, and strong attachment between rats and their owners are all covered in this comprehensive guide to housekeeping fancy rats.

BY
ERICA W. WILSON

TABLE OF CONTENTS:

CHAPTER 1: OVERVIEW OF FANCY RATS

Rattus norvegicus domestica is the scientific name for the fancy rat, which is a domesticated brown rat. This amazing critter has evolved over generations from being thought of as a nuisance to being one of the most adored little pets in the world. Fancy rats are gregarious, clean, clever, and loving creatures who flourish in human company. Examining their history of domestication, how they vary from their wild ancestors, and their attractiveness to contemporary pet owners are all necessary to comprehend their journey, traits, and popularity.

The 18th and 19th centuries saw the start of the serious domestication of rats. Wild brown rats were widespread in European towns at the period, when they flourished in food storage facilities, alleys, and sewers. Human fascination with rats gradually emerged, despite the fact that they were typically feared and despised, especially during times like the Black Death when they were mistakenly accused of transmitting plague (now understood to be transmitted by fleas on rats). The first fancy rats originated from the more unusual-looking or amiable animals that rat catchers sometimes retained and reared. In addition to being bred for distinctive colors and characteristics, these rats were employed in blood sports like rat-baiting, a brutal and now prohibited activity. The early domestication that resulted in the contemporary fancy rat was prompted by some people's appreciation of these rodents' unique looks and intriguing personalities.

In Victorian England, Jack Black, the Royal Rat Catcher, was among the earliest well-known rat breeders. He was well-known for gathering and raising rats of various hues, particularly those with peculiar temperaments or patterns. He sold his "fancy rats" to women in Queen Victoria's court as well as to other people in London, who caged them, appreciated their beauty, and even taught them. By transforming the rat from a simple annoyance to a possible friend, this early movement influenced public opinion.

In England, fancy rats had started to show up at pet exhibitions by the late 19th and early 20th centuries. In 1901, the National Mouse Club held the first known rat exhibition. Rat keeping started to become accepted as a pastime after this incident, which was a watershed. Rats gradually gained popularity as pets due to their intelligence and softer nature, even if mice were still the most popular pet rodent at the time. In 1976, the UK saw the founding of the National Fancy Rat Society (NFRS), which contributed to the formalization of color classifications, breeding standards, and pet care recommendations. Similar clubs and organizations later arose in the US, establishing the fancy rat as a respectable pet.

Fancy rats differ from their wild counterparts in many ways than just disposition and color. Although the general anatomy of domesticated rats may be similar to that of wild brown rats, they are often smaller, have a far wider variety of coat colors, and behave much more submissively. Fancy rats are developed especially for their calm, amiable temperaments and social adaptability, while wild rats are often defensive or jittery and are suspicious of people. In addition to enjoying touching and seeking out human contact, fancy rats may also display love by grooming, snuggling, or peacefully perching on their owner's shoulder.

Even the name "fancy rat" might be perplexing. It comes from the pastime of "animal fancying," which is the selective breeding of animals for certain qualities, much like dog or cat fanciers. It does not apply to rats that are "fancy" in the sense of being elegant or high-end. Clubs and societies now recognize a wide variety of fancy rats. These include rex rats, which have whiskers and curly fur; dumbo rats, who are identified by their enormous, low-set ears; hairless rats, which are developed specifically for their lack of fur; and standard rats, which have short, smooth coats and typical ear placement. The species may have a great range of looks because of the color patterns, which include hooded, Berkshire, Siamese, dalmatian, and many more.

Despite their differences, all fancy rats have some traits in common that make them wonderful pets. One of their most remarkable characteristics is their intellect. Fancy rats can solve basic puzzles, navigate mazes, learn tricks, and recognize their names. Like dogs or cats, they may form strong bonds with their human caretakers and can grow into unique individuals. While some rats are quiet and affectionate, others are gregarious and active. Since of their gregarious nature, rats make excellent companions for both humans and one another. However, since lonely rats may experience loneliness and sadness, it is best to keep them in pairs or small groups.

Another area where elegant rats transcend unfavorable perceptions is cleanliness. Domesticated rats groom themselves often, sometimes as much as cats, defying the stereotype that they are filthy creatures. When given the proper conditions, they are meticulous about their dwelling area and maintain immaculate fur. A rat's cage may stay odor-free and clean with the right care and the use of safe, non-odorous bedding.

Fancy rats have grown in popularity as pets in homes all around the globe in recent decades, especially in North America and Europe. Their favorable qualities, simplicity of maintenance, and adaptability for compact living areas like flats are among the factors contributing to their growing appeal. Furthermore, rats provide an alluring substitute that nonetheless offers robust contact and affection, as more individuals get disenchanted with conventional pets like dogs and cats because of issues with space, money, or lifestyle.

Rats are also common in educational settings, where they are sometimes housed in classrooms to educate kids in biology, empathy, and responsibility. Rats appreciate being handled and may develop strong ties with many individuals, in contrast to hamsters, who are often more isolated and less social. As long as adult supervision is in place to guarantee careful handling and proper maintenance, this makes them perfect for group situations or families with kids.

Rat keeping is not without its difficulties, however. For owners who get attached, their comparatively brief lifespan, usually two to three years, can be emotionally taxing. Additionally, they are susceptible to certain diseases, such tumors and respiratory infections, especially if they are not bred properly. As a result, it's imperative that potential owners look into trustworthy breeders or adopt from rat rescues that place a high value on the animals' disposition and general health.

To sum up, the elegant rat is an amazing illustration of how human perceptions of animals may change over time. The rat, formerly vilified and feared, has gained a particular place in the hearts of pet owners who value its charm, intellect, and devotion. The fancy rat has a long history of domestication, a wide range of physical characteristics, and a highly gregarious and trainable behavior, all of which contribute to its increasing popularity as a premium companion animal. More individuals are learning to love owning rats and realizing that these little animals provide tremendous benefits in return as knowledge grows and prejudices fade.

CHAPTER 2: THE FANCY RAT'S PHYSICAL FEATURES

The look of fancy rats is as varied as their personalities. Due to years of careful breeding, fanciers have created a variety of morphological characteristics that set these rats apart from their wild counterparts and make them attractive. The main physical traits of the fancy rat are examined in this chapter, including its size, weight, and longevity; its many coat types; its vast range of color and patterns; and the distinction between Dumbo and regular ear placements. Each of these characteristics influences how rats are categorized and valued in the pet and show industries in addition to their looks.

Lifespan, Weight, and Size:

Medium-sized rodents, fancy rats usually have bodies between 9 and 11 inches long, and their tails may be almost as long as their bodies. Adult male rats are much bigger, averaging 450 to 650 grams (1 to 1.4 pounds), however some may become considerably heavier depending on nutrition and heredity. Adult female rats typically weigh between 250 and 450 grams (approximately 0.5 to 1 pound).

Despite being smaller than dogs or cats, fancy rats have strong, muscular bodies that are a reflection of their busy lives. While girls are often more thin and nimble, men are typically stockier and more sturdy. In addition to influencing housing choices and interpersonal patterns, this size disparity becomes apparent early in their development.

Sadly, compared to many other pets, fancy rats have a limited lifetime. Fancy rats typically live 2 to 3 years, while some may live up to 4 years if given the right care and have the right genes. Although many potential owners find this short lifespan to be a drawback, it also fosters close, passionate relationships with the animal throughout its lifetime. A luxury rat may have a longer, healthier life if they are fed properly, have a clean habitat, are socialized, and have access to veterinary care.

Types of Coats:

The variety of coats on fancy rats is one of their most endearing characteristics. Breeders have created a variety of coat kinds, each with unique textures, requirements for maintenance, and visual attractiveness. These coat types are often used to classify individual rats in rat exhibitions and breed standards.

1. Smooth Coat Standard:
   The most prevalent and organic kind is the ordinary coat. It feels smooth and silky and rests flat on the body. This coat mimics the traditional appearance of a tamed rat and is simple to maintain. This coat is available in all recognizable hues and patterns and may be found on both men and females.

2. Rex: Rex rats often have curled whiskers and hair that is wavy or curly. They seem plush or woolly due to their coat's tendency to be thicker and coarser than a smooth coat. The degree of curliness in Rex coats varies greatly; some have tight curls, while others have a frizzy, ruffled appearance. A clue is the curled whiskers. Some rex rats may seem patchwork or less fluffy as they mature because their coat may weaken.

3. Double Rex: When two rex rats are bred together, a double rex is produced. These rats often have bald patches or patchy hair, giving them a distinctive "moth-eaten" appearance. Throughout their lives, they could experience hair loss and growth. Their whiskers are kinked or curled, much like the rex's, and their texture is often softer but more erratic.

4. Hairless: Rats without hair have very little or no fur. Their exposed skin has a warm, somewhat rubbery feel to it. They usually don't have a complete coat, however some could have a few whiskers or fuzz. Because they don't have fur, hairless rats are more likely to scratch, be sensitive to temperature changes, and have dry skin, therefore they need special attention. Despite their remarkable look, their increased care requirements make them unsuitable for everyone.

5. Satin: The coats of satin rats are very smooth and lustrous. Their fur has a shiny, somewhat metallic appearance because of the shine. This coat style is valued for its dramatic look in show settings and may come in any color or pattern. A hair structure that reflects light differently than regular fur is what gives the satin look.

There may be minor variations in grooming depending on the kind of coat. Depending on their surroundings and general health, certain rats, such as rex or hairless types, may need assistance with cleaning or moisturizing, even though the majority of rats are careful self-groomers.

Markings and Color Varieties:

The fancy rat's wide variety of colors and patterns is among its most striking features. Rats are often categorized using these genetically determined features in breeding programs and exhibits.

Among the most often used color types are:

The wild-type color Agouti has brownish fur with a mixture of brown, black, and gold hairs.

Black: Deep black fur that is solid.

Chocolate: A rich brown that often has a rosy or warm tone.

Siamese: Like the Siamese cat, this breed has a pale body with darker spots on the nose, foot, and base of the tail.

Blue: A chilly, steel-grey hue that is often regarded as uncommon and attractive.

Fawn: An eye-catching, cheery orangey-tan hue.

The rat's body's color placements and patterns are referred to as markings. Some popular and acknowledged marking kinds are as follows:

Hooded: The rat's head and shoulders are covered by a solid-colored "hood," with a band or stripe running down the back.

A solid-colored rat with a white belly and sometimes white feet or a white blaze on the snout is called a Berkshire.

Capped: The whole body is white, with just the top of the head being colored.

Blazed: Usually seen in conjunction with other marks, a white stripe runs down the nose.

Variegated: Patchy look due to irregular color splotches on a white background.

Certain rats may have distinctive patterns, including Masked (a color pattern that mimics a face mask) or Dalmatian (white with black markings). Fancy rats may have an almost infinite number of different appearances because of these combinations, each of which is unique and simple to identify.

Standard Ear Placement vs. Dumbo

The ear type of beautiful rats is one of their most distinctive and charming characteristics. Two main types exist:

1. **Standard Ear:** Rats with standard ears have ears on top of their heads, angled slightly to the sides. Both wild and farmed rats have this more prevalent ear type. They resemble typical rodents because of their medium-sized, erect ears.

The term "Dumbo Ear" refers to the enormous, spherical ears that are positioned lower on the sides of the skull of Dumbo rats. Because of this, they have a unique, cartoonish look that many owners find endearing. Dumbo rats' adorable, cuddly appearance is enhanced by their somewhat wider heads. The size and position of the ears are just cosmetic; they have no effect on the rat's hearing or general well-being.

Dumbo rats are a subspecies of fancy rats rather than a distinct breed. In order to generate Dumbo children, both parents must possess the recessive gene that causes Dumbo ears. They are popular with both pet owners and show fans because of their distinctive look.

In conclusion, fancy rats have a fascinating variety of physical traits that make them enjoyable to see and handle. Every fancy rat is a different person, with silky and curly coats, a variety of colors and patterns, sleek standard ears, and huge, low-set Dumbo ears. These variants honor the amazing variety that one of the most underappreciated companion animals in the world can provide via careful breeding and good care, in addition to appealing to human aesthetic tastes. The first step in being a considerate and knowledgeable rat owner is to comprehend and value these physical characteristics.

CHAPTER 3: FANCY RAT BEHAVIOR AND TEMPERAMENT

The exceptional behavior and temperament of fancy rats are among the strongest arguments for their popularity. Domesticated rats are smart, kind, and gregarious animals, quite different from their wild forebears in both look and disposition. They have complex emotional lives, show devotion, develop strong relationships with both people and other rats, and have intriguing but subtle communication styles. This chapter examines their intellect and social nature, their ability to show love, their playfulness and energy levels, and the ways in which they communicate via vocalizations and body language.

Social Intelligence and Nature

Fancy rats are very gregarious creatures. Rats live in intricate colonies in the wild that rely on communication, hierarchy, and teamwork. Their domesticated counterparts nevertheless possess this same social urge, which makes friendship crucial to their welfare. Because they need the continual contact, reciprocal grooming, and social structure that comes with living with their own kind, fancy rats thrive when kept in housing with at least one other rat, ideally of the same sex to prevent mating.

Even with frequent human contact, a rat living alone is likely to experience stress, loneliness, and depression. Behavioral problems including excessive chewing, aggressiveness, drowsiness, or over-grooming might result from these feelings. Rats like small groups or couples where they may interact, play, and snuggle. At least two rats should ideally be adopted simultaneously by their owners; these rats should ideally be littermates or have previously bonded.

Fascinatingly clever, fancy rats are also gregarious. New owners are often surprised by their trainability, recall, and problem-solving skills. Rats can run mazes, learn their names, react to vocal signals, and perform skills like retrieving things or leaping over hoops. They can even be trained to return to their cage when instructed to do so and to come when called. Because of their very flexible minds, they are often used in behavioral and scientific study.

Because they are intelligent, they also get bored rapidly if they are not given mental stimulation. Rats may get irritated and nervous in the absence of contact and enrichment. A healthy rat habitat must thus include toys, puzzles, climbing frames, and frequent playing outside of the cage. They take pleasure in engaging with their environment, changing their bedding, and investigating new items.

Love for Humans:

Fancy rats may be among the most loving tiny pets available, despite the traditional misconception that they are dirty or harmful. They often display their affection in charming ways after they have formed a link with their owner. They may burrow into your clothing, clamber onto your shoulder, lick your fingers (a grooming technique that resembles love), or even nip lightly, a gesture of satisfaction known as "bruxing."

Rats pick up on their owner's voice, smell, and daily schedule very rapidly. When they hear their name or the sound of you coming, many will approach the cage entrance. They may eventually get so attached to their owner that they anticipate contact with their human and show obvious symptoms of delight when they do.

Patience and positive reinforcement are necessary to establish this attachment, particularly with young or timid rats. Treats, a calm voice, and consistent, gentle handling help them link humans to rewards and safety. Fancy rats often appreciate physical intimacy after trust has been established. They may sleep on your lap, wrap up in your sweatshirt, or even "groom" your face or hands as they would a cage mate.

Rats seek for emotional connection, in contrast to many tiny pets that are mostly lonely or distant. Many rat owners say that their pets appear to read emotions and provide calm company when their person is feeling worried or depressed. Rats also appreciate being a part of a family.

Levels of Playfulness and Activity:

Playfulness comes easily to fancy rats. Young rats perform chase games and pretend battles in the wild, and domesticated rats bring this joyful spirit into their homes. Rats engage in play with both people and other rats, exhibiting their happy dispositions by bouncing, wrestling, and actively exploring.

Generally speaking, they are moderately to highly active, particularly in the morning and evening. Rats are crepuscular, which means that dawn and dusk are when they are most active. Because the rats will often be prepared for engagement in the morning before work or school and again in the evening, they are thus a perfect fit for persons with typical daily schedules.

You may see frequent tumble or chasing activities among a couple or group of rats. Rats engage in this innocuous activity as a necessary component of their exercise and sociability. They also play with toys; climbing towers, tunnels, rope ladders, and chewing blocks are particularly well-liked. Some rats even pick up skills like fetching, playing tag, and handling tiny things like reward dispensers and puzzle balls.

Rats need time outside of their cages every day to maintain mental and physical stimulation. For them to explore and engage with their humans, a secure, enclosed play space devoid of cables or potentially hazardous items is ideal. Many rats like to go through tunnels, climb on furniture, or just lie on their owner and watch TV or read at this time.

Comprehending Vocalizations and Body Language:

Rats use a wide variety of intricate body language and noises to communicate. Recognizing these cues enables owners to identify the personalities, wants, and emotional states of pet rats.

The language of the body:

Bruxing: A gentle teeth-grinding that often accompanies a sluggish eye movement known as "boggling." Bruxing is an indication of relaxation or satisfaction.
Boggling is the term for when the eyeballs vibrate quickly, usually as a result of intense bruxing. Although it may seem shocking, this is a very typical way to demonstrate delight.
Grooming: Rats groom others and themselves to be clean and affectionate. The act of a rat grooming its human is a symbol of connection and trust.

Puffing up fur: A sign that the rat is sick, scared, or chilly. In males, puffing may also indicate territorial behavior.

Freezing: When a rat is frightened or feels threatened, it will abruptly stop moving. It's a natural reaction to danger.

Wrestling: Young and even adult rats often engage in this play activity. Unless there is squeaking, bleeding, or chasing, which might be signs of dominance issues, it is mostly innocuous.

Vocalizations:

The majority of rat vocalizations are ultrasonic, meaning that the human ear cannot pick them up. Nonetheless, you can hear the following noises:

Squeaking: May be a sign of discomfort, anxiety, or a dispute for control.

Chirping or clucking: When playing or exploring, some rats will produce joyful, enthusiastic chirps.

Sneezing or sniffling: Regular sneezing should be watched for as it may be a sign of a respiratory issue.

Additionally, rats use nonverbal clues including posture, facial expressions, and tail movement to communicate. Most owners eventually become adept at "reading" their rats, recognizing changes in behavior, mood, or health.

In conclusion, one of the most alluring aspects of fancy rats is their temperament and demeanor. They transcend the unfavorable perceptions that still exist in certain areas since they are gregarious, clever, loving, and fun. They communicate in complex, subtle ways, provide hours of amusement and affection, and develop close relationships with both their human caretakers and other rats. These animals prove to be some of the most fascinating and emotionally engaged pets one can own with the right knowledge and attention. Not only is their conduct fascinating, but it also demonstrates the strength of domestication and the closeness that can be formed between people and animals.

CHAPTER 4: SELECTING AND PURCHASING A FANCY RAT

It's thrilling and fulfilling to bring a luxury rat into your house, but it's crucial to start the process with thorough preparation and well-informed choices. Selecting healthy rats from reliable sources, being aware of the telltale indications of a good breeder or rescue, figuring out when a rat is ready for adoption, learning how to properly sex your rats, and making sure you adopt in suitable groups are the first stages in responsible rat ownership. Rats should never live alone since they are very gregarious creatures. In order to guarantee your long-term happiness as a rat parent and the welfare of your fancy rats, this chapter will walk you through every step of the process.

Choosing Healthy Rats from Rescues or Breeders:

The source from which you choose to adopt your fancy rats has a big impact on their life expectancy, disposition, and general health. Pet store-bought rats are often produced in rodent factories with no consideration for socialization, temperament, or genetic health. Even while some rats from pet stores make excellent friends, it is far more ethical and dependable to get your rats from a respectable breeder or a devoted rescue group.

Reputable breeders put their rats' temperament, health, and heritage first. In order to increase favorable features, eradicate inherited disorders, and raise well-socialized animals in hygienic, stimulating habitats, they often breed selectively. A breeder needs to respond to your inquiries, be open and honest about their breeding methods, and provide assistance long after adoption. Before permitting an adoption, the top breeders may even conduct an interview or inquire about your setup since they are concerned about the whereabouts of their rats.

A further great source is rat rescues. Numerous organizations accept unwanted, abandoned, or surrendered rats and use socialization, veterinary treatment, and appropriate care to rehabilitate them. In addition to saving a life, adopting from a rescue lessens the strain of population growth. With the correct patience and care, rescue rats of any age may still become devoted companions. Adopting bonded couples or groups is another excellent use for rescues.

Regardless of the origin of your rats, healthy rats need to exhibit certain behavioral and physical characteristics:

 Clean ears and nose Smooth, well-groomed fur (unless hairless or red) Dry and clean tail and bottom, Bright, clear eyes without discharge, Curiosity and energy, Normal breathing without wheezing, clicking, or exertion.

Rats who are sluggish, bent over, sneezy, or scratching excessively should be avoided since these might be signs of mites or respiratory diseases.

Qualifications for a Trustworthy Source:

To make sure your rats have the greatest start in life, choose a reliable breeder or rescue. The following are crucial signs of a reliable source:

1. The environment's cleanliness
The rats' living quarters should be odor-free, dry, and clean whether you're at a rescue facility or a breeder's house. There should be plenty of food, nesting materials, and enrichment in well-maintained cages.

2. Socialization Reputable rats should be handled on a regular basis and made to feel at ease in human company. Observe their interactions; do they come to you with interest? Do they accept being lifted? Early socialization has a significant influence on behavior in the long run.

3. Transparency and Knowledge
Rat health, breeding history, and care should all be well-known to a reputable breeder or rescue worker. When you inquire about the origins, parentage, or medical history of the rats (in the case of breeders or rescues), they ought to be happy to answer your queries.

4. Adoption Guidelines
Reputable rescues and breeders often conduct interviews or adoption applications. They will give preference to adopting rats out in suitable pairs or groups, and they won't sell single rats unless you already have another rat at home.

5. Post-Adoption Assistance

Reputable sources provide direction and follow-up. They are pleased to respond to inquiries after adoption and want their rats to thrive in their new homes.

Steer clear of any vendor or breeder who:

Offers to export rats without screening; is unable to provide information about the rat's past; keeps animals in filthy or overcrowded cages; breeds excessively without any clear objectives or attention to health; and is prepared to sell a single rat to a person who has no other rats.

How to Sex Your Rats and When to Adopt Them:

Usually, fancy rats are 6 to 8 weeks old when they are ready for adoption. They are now consuming solid food, have started to have their own personalities, and have been weaned off of their moms. Adopted rats that are too young (less than five weeks) may not have the correct socialization, may not receive the mother's vital nutrients, and may have behavioral development issues. Adopted older rats may need more time to connect, particularly if they haven't been handled much, but with patience, they may still develop into loving, dependable companions.

It's important to know how to sex your rats, especially to prevent unintended breeding. Rats that are male and female should not be kept together unless one or both of them have been spayed or neutered.

By around five weeks of age, the testicles of male rats (bucks) are visible. They are noticeable and often simple to identify. Additionally, males often have a larger gap between the genital entrance and the anus.

The vaginal hole of female rats (does) is closer to the anus, and their testicles are not visible. Small nipples may also be seen around the abdomen of adult females.

A knowledgeable breeder or rescue worker should be able to sex the rats for you if you're not sure. When adopting, it's wise to be sure, particularly if you're getting many rats from various litters.
Rats shouldn't live alone, thus it's important to choose compatible companions.

Rats are sociable creatures and should never live alone is perhaps the most essential guideline in rat ownership. Over time, a lone rat will experience loneliness, boredom, and melancholy regardless of how much human engagement it gets. They depend on one another for protection, play, grooming, and sleep since they are hardwired to live in groups.

Adopting rats in pairs or trios of the same sex is ideal. Since they have already formed a relationship and have grown up together, littermates are often the ideal choice. To guarantee compatibility and avoid fighting, appropriate introduction protocols must be followed when adopting adults or combining rats from various origins.

Here are some basic tips for pairing:

Male plus Male: This combination usually works well as long as the males are introduced correctly and don't take control. Older men are often more relaxed.
In general, females and females are quite successful, particularly if they are adopted together at an early age. Women tend to be more vivacious and talkative.

Young + Old: Because older rats are often more tolerant, it might be beneficial to introduce a younger rat to an older one. However, throughout the bonding process, more oversight is required.

Steer clear of:

Rats may breed quickly and in large numbers, therefore unless they are neutered or spayed, they should be housed males and females together.

Leaving one rat alone, even for a short time. If a rat dies, think about getting a new friend right away.

The rescue should assist you in adopting a second rat or guiding you through the introduction procedure with your current rats if you are adopting a single rat from a rescue because it arrived alone.

Finally,

There is more to selecting and obtaining elegant rats than just choosing the prettiest face at the pet shop. It calls for careful preparation, ethical sourcing, and a thorough comprehension of their emotional and social requirements. Your pets have a higher chance of living long, happy lives if you choose healthy rats from moral breeders or rescues. The foundation for a fulfilling relationship between you and your rats is laid by learning how to sex them correctly, adopting them when they're ready, and above all making sure they have company. The adoption process, when handled carefully, is the beginning of a loving, educational, and joyful relationship.

CHAPTER 5: THE FANCY RAT'S ENVIRONMENT AND HOUSING

One of the most crucial duties of ownership for fancy rats is to provide a cozy, engaging, and secure living environment. Rats are gregarious, inquisitive, and highly clever creatures who flourish in settings that replicate their innate tendencies to explore, climb, burrow, and nest. Their general pleasure, mental stimulation, and physical health are all enhanced by a suitable living arrangement. Conversely, substandard living may result in boredom, tension, hostility, and even health issues. The main components of rat housing are examined in this chapter, including cage size and arrangement, bar levels and spacing, secure bedding, and the use of enrichment items such toys, tunnels, and hammocks.

Optimal Cage Dimensions and Configuration:

Because they are energetic creatures, fancy rats need plenty of room to roam, explore, and socialize. Although bigger is always preferable, the ideal cage size for two rats should provide at least 2 cubic feet of room per rat. For a pair of rats, a cage that is at least 30 inches long, 18 inches wide, and 24 inches high is often advised. Cages should be proportionately bigger for larger groupings.

Rats do not do well in compact, one-story cages as mice or hamsters do. Since they are naturally climbers, their cages need to contain both floor space and height to accommodate vertical mobility. Multiple-level cages, platforms, and ramps provide them the chance to climb and exercise, two activities that are essential to their health.

Rats want solitude and exploration, which should be reflected in the layout of their cage. It ought to contain:

Climbing opportunities such as ropes, ladders, or platforms Burrowing options such as a thick layer of bedding or dig boxes Nesting areas for sleeping and hiding Open areas for food, drink, and social contact

A well-designed cage helps keep them from becoming bored or frustrated by simulating the diversity they would encounter in their natural habitat. Rats should never be kept in unenriched bare metal cages, tubs, or basic aquariums since this causes mental stress and bad health.

Bar spacing and multi-level cages:

For fancy rats, multi-level cages are great. They assist keep the rats busy and engaged by using vertical space and providing them with extra room to explore. Safe ramps or climbing structures may be used to link levels, and unique elements can be included into each level, such as separate areas for play, sleeping, and food and water.

Take into account the following while choosing or constructing a multi-level cage:

Platforms should be firm or coated with fleece to minimize foot injuries. Ramps should have traction to prevent slippage. The distances between levels should be sufficiently wide to allow for simple mobility, but not so wide that a rat may trip and get injuries.

Bar spacing is still another important factor. Rats can fit through narrow spaces and are very adaptable. There should be no more space between the bars than:

1/4 inch (0.64 cm) for youngsters or smaller breeds of rats, and 1/2 inch (1.27 cm) for adults.

An excessively wide bar spacing presents a significant escape danger. Although vertical bars are OK, horizontal bars are preferable as they make climbing possible. If there is wire mesh flooring, they should be avoided or covered with fleece or solid material to avoid injuries like bumblefoot, which is a painful ailment brought on by pressure on the foot soles.

Powder-coated metal cages are long-lasting and hygienic. Steer clear of hardwood cages that retain urine and are difficult to clean, or plastic cages with little ventilation.

Bedding and Substrate Safety:

Your choice of bedding or substrate is critical for respiratory health and comfort. Certain bedding materials may emit hazardous dust or oils, and rats' respiratory systems are delicate.

Options for safe bedding include:

Paper-based bedding, such as Kaytee Clean & Cozy and Carefresh, is dust-free, soft, and absorbent.
Aspen shavings are a safe wood-based bedding that is comparatively odorless and dust-free.
Fleece liners: Soft underfoot, reusable, and machine-washable fabric. often used on platforms or solid cage flooring.
Hemp bedding: Rat owners are increasingly choosing this low-dust, environmentally beneficial solution.

Steer clear of the following materials:

The aromatic oils included in pine and cedar shavings have the potential to harm the liver and respiratory system.
Cat litter made of clay: too dusty and might make breathing difficult.
Corn cob bedding: Frequently moldy and insufficiently absorbent.

Spot cleaning should be done every day to get rid of filthy material, and bedding should be replaced at least once a week. A clean cage lowers the chance of parasites, respiratory illnesses, and ammonia accumulation while maintaining a healthy habitat.

Your rats' natural need to burrow may be satiated by providing a digging box or deep bedding area. To make foraging enjoyable, you may even conceal snacks or torn paper within.

Toys, Hammocks, and Tunnels for Enrichment:

Rats are intelligent, inquisitive creatures that need daily mental and physical stimulation. They may become obese, depressed, and engage in harmful activities if they are not given enough stimulation. Thankfully, improving their surroundings is simple and enjoyable.

Tubes and Tunnels:

Rats like exploring hidey-holes, crawl spaces, and tunnels. These provide them a feeling of security and replicate their natural burrowing habit. One may construct tunnels out of:

PVC pipes Cardboard mailing tubes Sewn fabric tunnels Plastic ferret tubes.

To provide a fascinating habitat, they may be hung or placed along cage floors and changed on a regular basis.

Bedding and Hammocks:

Rats love their hammocks! They are used as places to sleep and relax when hung from the cage's walls or roof. They are available in a variety of styles:

Corner bunkers, Flat hammocks, Pocket hammocks, Fleece cubes or hanging tents.

Because rats often urinate on hammocks, they should be cleaned once a week. Particularly during the colder months, fabric bedding offers comfort and warmth.

Toys and Tools for Foraging:

Toys that stimulate the brains and test the ability to solve problems are highly favored by fancy rats. Favorites include:

Chew toys made of untreated wood; puzzle feeders and snuffle mats; foraging balls that release rewards; cardboard boxes with holes cut into them; and climbing ropes and ladders.

To prevent kids from becoming bored, switch up the toys often. Rotate them once a week or every few days to ensure that the surroundings are always fresh.

Equipment for Climbing and Exercise:

Rats like to climb, so think about including:

Rope nets, climbing walls, ladders, and hanging platforms.

For daily play sessions, some owners construct ornate "rat gyms" either within or outside the cage.

Toys should never have tiny pieces, sharp edges, or hazardous ingredients; they should always be rat-safe. Keep an eye on out-of-cage play, particularly in unrat-proofed areas.

Conclusion:

Because fancy rats are gregarious, energetic, and clever animals, their home and surroundings should be tailored to meet their specific demands. The basis for a happy, healthy existence is a large, multi-level cage with secure bedding and a range of enrichment activities. Everything from chew toys and climbing ropes to tunnels and hammocks shapes their everyday experience. In addition to thriving physiologically, fancy rats that are kept in the right environment also grow more playful, friendly, and involved. Carefully planning a habitat is essential to the welfare of these amazing tiny friends, not simply a luxury.

CHAPTER 6: DIET AND NUTRITION

One of the most important aspects of rat care is feeding your beautiful rat a meal that is balanced and suitable for its species. Their longevity, coat quality, immune system, and energy levels are all impacted by proper diet. Rats are opportunistic omnivores, which means they consume a variety of foods in the wild. Similar dietary requirements apply to domestic fancy rats, and to maintain their health and activity levels, their meals should include a mix of vital minerals, vitamins, fiber, and water.

The elements of a healthy rat diet are described in this chapter, along with foods to avoid, safe rewards for training and enrichment, and the best ways to schedule feedings and provide water.

Basics of a Balanced Diet: Protein, Fresh Produce, and Lab Blocks

Three key ingredients make up a healthy rat diet:

1. Superior Lab Pellets or Blocks

The foundation of a well-balanced rat diet is lab blocks, often known as rodent blocks or rat pellets. These are specifically designed to avoid selective feeding, in which rats may choose just their favorite foods from a varied meal and overlook vital nutrients, and to provide steady nourishment in each mouthful.

Seek out lab blocks that have:

4–6% fat, 14–16% protein, A source of digestive fiber.

Oxbow Regal Rat, Mazuri Rat & Mouse Diet, and Science Selective Rat Food are all reputable products. Steer clear of inferior products that include a lot of sugar, artificial coloring, or fillers.

To promote foraging behavior, distribute lab blocks throughout the cage or place them in a dish.

2. Fresh Produce

Vital vitamins, minerals, antioxidants, and hydration are all found in fresh fruits and vegetables. To prevent imbalances and upset stomachs, they should only comprise 10–20% of the rat's daily diet.

Vegetables that are safe to eat (ideally served raw or mildly steamed):

Green beans, Broccoli, Carrots, Cucumber, Bell peppers, Zucchini, Kale, Moderate spinach, Romaine lettuce (not iceberg).

Fruits that are safe (serve in limited quantities because of their sugar content):

Bananas, Melon, Mango, Pears, Apples (seedless), Berries (strawberries, blueberries, and raspberries).

Always produce a good wash and remove any potentially dangerous or difficult-to-digest seeds, pits, or rinds.

3. Nutritious Proteins

Rats, particularly young or pregnant females, need some animal protein. Although most individuals can get enough protein from lab blocks, tiny quantities of extra protein may sometimes be provided.

Sources of healthy protein:

Cooked egg (boiled or scrambled); Unseasoned cooked chicken or turkey; Tofu; Plain yogurt (in small quantities); Mealworms (as snacks).

Adults should only have protein snacks two or three times a week. In older rats, particularly males, too much protein may cause renal stress.

Items to Steer Clear of (Toxic or Dangerous)

Rats should never eat some foods since they are poisonous or dangerous. Some are simply toxic, while others are detrimental to their digestive systems.

Hazardous or Toxic Foods:

The d-limonene found in citrus fruits, particularly oranges for male rats, may have an adverse effect on the kidneys of male rats.
Chocolate: poisonous since it contains theobromine.
The neurological system is overstimulated by caffeine.
Carbonated drinks: rats are prone to gas accumulation and are unable to burp.
Uncooked peanuts or beans contain toxins and anti-nutrients.
Raw potatoes or green potato skin contain harmful substances.

Excessive use of onions and garlic might result in blood problems.

Rats are very susceptible to mycotoxins, so avoid eating anything that has mold on it.

Choking hazards include sticky foods like peanut butter (unless diluted).

Iceberg lettuce: low in nutrients and prone to diarrhea.

Before introducing any new food, be sure it is safe for rats by checking again.

Training Incentives and Safe Treats:

Treats play a significant role in enrichment, training, and bonding. They provide diversity to the rat's experience, promote trust, and reward good behavior when used sparingly.

Inspiring Healthy Treats:

Plain Cheerios or cooked oats (in modest quantities)
Cooked brown rice or pasta Peas or corn kernels A little slice of cheese (infrequently) Unsweetened cereal (low in sugar)
Low-sugar baby food without garlic or onions Moderate amounts of dried bananas or apples

These goodies may be used to train tricks, entice your rats to come when called, or help them get into carriers for transportation. Rats may readily acquire weight, and obesity causes a number of health problems, so avoid giving them too many sweets.

Treat tip: Always provide a reward for actions you want to encourage, such using a litter box, stepping onto your hand, or going back to a cage.

Water Access and Feeding Schedule:

Rats may often munch all day and all night, but they thrive on a regular feeding schedule. Since rats are crepuscular, feeding is most effective in the early morning and evening when they are most active.

Lab blocks should be supplied once a day in enough quantities or at all times.
It is recommended that rats get tiny portions of fresh food and snacks once a day, usually in the evening when they are more active.

Steer clear of giving rats unrestricted access to high-calorie fruits or snacks since this might cause obesity and decrease their desire for nutritious food.

Access to Water:

Fresh, clean water must always be accessible. Because bowls are prone to tipping and contamination, the best sanitary choice is a water bottle with a sipper tube.

Advice:

Every day, make sure the bottle isn't leaking or blocked, and refill it with new water.
Use a bottle brush or warm, soapy water to clean the bottle once a week.

For versatility, some owners choose to supply both a bottle and a water dish, particularly for elderly or ill rats who may find it difficult to use bottles.

Conclusion:

A deliberate, well-balanced meal is the first step to a fancy rat's health and happiness. Their diet should consist mostly of high-quality lab blocks, with occasional protein and little amounts of fresh fruits and vegetables as supplements. In order to maintain a healthy weight, treats should be given sparingly, even if they are beneficial for bonding and training. Toxic foods may save your rat's life, so it's just as vital to know what you don't feed as what you do. The key components of healthy rat nutrition are a regular feeding schedule and simple access to fresh water. You may encourage vigor, increase your rats' lifetime, and improve the quality of your time together by carefully attending to their nutritional demands.

CHAPTER 7: FANCY RAT HEALTH AND COMMON ILLNESSES

A long and happy life for your fancy rat depends on keeping it healthy. Although rats are often resilient creatures, they may develop some health problems, just like any other pet. Because of their tiny size, fast metabolism, and gregarious nature, infections may spread among cagemates if they are not detected and treated in a timely manner. Any rat owner may feel more confident and competent in promoting their pet's well-being if they know the symptoms of excellent health, frequent ailments, the value of exotic animal doctors, and how to provide appropriate preventive treatment.

Healthy Rat Indications:

It's crucial to understand the appearance and behavior of a healthy rat in order to spot problems when they arise. Rats are lively, vigilant, and curious when given the right care. The following indicators will be present in a healthy fancy rat:

Clear, bright eyes (no discharge or dullness) Clean ears and nose (no crusting or excessive porphyrin (red tears) Smooth, glossy coat (no bald spots or scabs) Normal breathing (silent, no wheezing or clicking) Active and alert behavior, especially in the evenings Good appetite and regular water intake Strong, well-coordinated movement, Clean genital and tail areas with no indications of soiling or inflammation.

By observing your rats every day, you may create a baseline of typical behavior that will make it simpler to spot any deviations early on.

Typical Health Issues:

Even with the greatest of intentions, fancy rats might develop certain health issues. Some of the most common problems are listed below:

1. Infections of the Respiratory System

Because of their sensitive respiratory systems, rats are particularly vulnerable to upper and lower respiratory infections, which may develop into chronic conditions.

Among the symptoms are:

Lethargy Loss of appetite Nasal discharge or "red tears" around the eyes and nose Sneezing, wheezing, or hard breathing

Bacterial infections like Mycoplasma pulmonis are often the source of respiratory problems, which may become worse when exposed to stress, dust, or poor air quality. They are usually treated with antibiotics and need to be seen by a veterinarian.

2. Tumors, particularly those of the breast

Older rats, particularly females, often develop tumors. They may develop quickly and obstruct internal organs or mobility, even though many are benign (non-cancerous).

Indications:

Distinct under-skin lumps, usually on the sides or abdomen, Alterations in movement or personal hygiene, Abrupt weight increase in one region.

The key is early detection. Many rats can be surgically removed, but not all of them are suitable candidates because of their age or overall condition.

3. Parasites and Mites:

Extreme itching and irritation may be brought on by external parasites like lice or mites.

Symptoms:

Hair loss or bald patches Restlessness or irritability Scratching Scabs, particularly on the shoulders or behind the ears

Usually, oral or topical anti-parasitic drugs are used to treat them. Since mites may remain in bedding and accessories, it's critical to thoroughly clean the whole cage if they are present.

4. Wounds and Abscesses

Rats that are bitten, scratched, or come into contact with foreign things may develop abscesses. These are pus-filled, bloated, and often heated bumps.

Indications:

Swelling Localized discomfort or heat Pus discharge in the event of a rupture

Typically, antibiotics and abscess drainage are part of the treatment.

5. Misalignment of the teeth, or malocclusion

A rat's teeth never stop growing. Overgrown incisors and trouble chewing might result from misalignment caused by improper wear down.

Indicators:

Weight loss, Difficulty chewing or losing food, Drooling.

In these situations, veterinary trimming is required, and recurrence may be avoided with routine dental monitoring.

6. Weakness in the Hind Leg (HLW)

HLW, a progressive decrease of hindlimb muscle tone and coordination, is typical in aged rats.

Indications:

Having trouble ascending; dragging the rear legs; and having thinner hindquarters.

Although there is no cure, supportive care such as improved cage access, pain management if needed, and high-nutrition foods can help manage it.

Exotic Vets Are Important:

Not all veterinarians are qualified to treat rats since they are regarded as exotic pets. The unique anatomy, ailments, and quantities of medications that are suitable for rodents may be unfamiliar to a typical veterinarian who treats dogs and cats.

The need of an exotic veterinarian:

Accurately identifying and treating diseases unique to rats Safe surgical procedures (such as tumor excision or spay/neuter) Appropriate medication dose and administration techniques Knowledge of rat behavior and distress indicators:

Before you need an exotic veterinarian in an emergency, it's a good idea to find one nearby. Establish a rapport early on by bringing your rats in for routine examinations. Make sure the veterinarian has knowledge of small animals, or rats in particular.

Health and Hygiene Prevention:

Cleanliness and proper husbandry may avoid or reduce a number of rat health problems. Promoting long-term health and vitality is the goal of prevention, not only halting disease.

1. Cleanliness of the cage

Do a weekly comprehensive cage clean, which includes cleaning all surfaces, toys, hammocks, and water bottles. Spot-clean every day by clearing away dirty bedding, excrement, and uneaten food.

Use gentle cleansers that are suitable for pets; stay away from ammonia and harsh chemicals.

2. Quality of Air

Keep cages out of bright sunlight and drafts, and steer clear of dusty bedding like pine or cedar. Avoid using aerosol sprays, smoking, or strong smells in the room.

3. Appropriate Nutrition

Provide a wholesome diet to boost immunological function (see Chapter 6). Limiting sweets and promoting exercise can help prevent obesity.

4. Place New Rats in Quarantine

Before adding additional rats to your existing group, always keep them apart for two to three weeks. This prevents sickness from spreading and allows you to watch for symptoms of illness in the newcomer.

5. Exercise and Enrichment

Rats that get stimulation are happier and healthier. The immune system may be weakened by stress and boredom. Every day, provide social contact, toys, and climbing structures.

6. Routine Health Examinations

Perform health examinations once a week:

Examine teeth and nails for parasites, scabs, or lumps. Keep an eye out for variations in behavior, weight, or breathing.

Early detection of minor issues can prevent emergencies.

Conclusion:

Fancy rats need careful, proactive care to be healthy and live a long life. Knowing the symptoms of common diseases and the telltale characteristics of a healthy rat can help you treat them promptly or seek veterinarian assistance. Numerous health problems may be avoided before they start by selecting a skilled exotic veterinarian, keeping your home clean, giving your rats a balanced diet, and routinely checking on them. Your care and attention to detail may significantly enhance your rat's quality of life, even if some issues like tumors or aging are unavoidable. A well-maintained fancy rat may live up to three years, and when you prioritize your well-being, each day of that existence will be more enjoyable for you both.

CHAPTER 8: TRAINING AND SOCIALIZATION

An important part of caring for fancy rats is socialization and training. These perceptive, sensitive creatures flourish when they are able to bond with both other rats and their human caretakers. A well-socialized rat will be more laid-back, loving, and self-assured in addition to being simpler to handle and care for. Building trust with your rat, hand-taming and bonding with them, teaching them basic skills and training (including litter habits), and dealing with behavioral problems like shyness or aggressiveness are all covered in this chapter.

Creating a Bond with Your Rat:

The sensation of bonding with a luxury rat is very satisfying. Being gregarious animals, these rodents develop close bonds with their people. Rats, however, may be initially hesitant or wary especially in a new environment because they are prey animals by nature.

Important bonding procedures:

When bringing your rats home for the first time, let them a full day or two to explore their cage and acclimate to their new environment without pressuring them to socialize.

2. Be present: Take a seat close to the cage and talk quietly. Let them smell through the bars at your hand. This makes it easier for them to identify your voice and fragrance.

3. Use food and treats: To create favorable associations with your presence, have snacks like berries, peas, or oats on hand.

Cage interaction: Put your hand inside the cage gently and let them come to you at their own speed. Do not corner or grasp them.

5. Consistent handling: After they are at ease, start lifting and holding them in both hands, one supporting the rear legs and the other under the chest. Initial sessions should be brief and mild.

6. Predictability and routine: Rats are routine creatures. Building trust and familiarity involves feeding, playing, and handling at the same time every day.

Depending on the rat's age, temperament, and upbringing, bonding might take a few days to several weeks.

Building Trust and Hand-Taming:

Teaching a rat to identify your hands with comfort, safety, and constructive engagement is known as hand-taming.

Hand-taming steps:

Begin small: Place your hand inside the cage and let the rat willingly crawl over it. Do not grasp from above, since this imitates the movement of a predator.

Reward curiosity: Give your rat a reward and praise each time it touches or walks on your hand.

Make time for connecting outside the cage: Provide a secure area for your rats to explore outside of their cage, such as a sofa or playpen. Allow them to climb on you while you sit calmly.

Avoid chasing: An anxious rat should never be chased or violently grabbed. Instead, use gentle gestures and sweets to entice them.

Have patience: Rats that have had little or bad human interaction need time to develop trust.

Your rat will eventually get used to being petted, lifted, and carried on your lap or shoulder.

Litter Training and Basic Tricks:

Like dogs and cats, fancy rats are very clever and can pick up basic habits and directions. The secret is positive reinforcement: provide food, compliments, or love to reward desired behavior.

Elementary Skills Rats Can Acquire:

1. Come when called: Prior to giving a reward, make a steady sound (such as a click, name, or whistle). Repeat often.

2. Twirl or spin: Lead your rat in a circle while holding a reward. As they follow the action, say "spin," and then give them a reward.

3. Stand up (beg): Say "stand" while holding a goodie over their head. When they raise themselves onto their rear legs, give them a reward.

4. Fetch: With experience, some rats may hunt and return tiny objects, such as paper balls.

5. Go into carrier or hand: To make transportation simpler, teach them to jump onto your hand or inside a travel cage.

To prevent weariness, always workout in quick bursts of five to ten minutes. Consistent, relaxed repetition and incentives work best for rats.

Training with Litter:

Rats have an innate preference for certain places for urinating and defecating. This inclination may be used to teach them to use a litter box.

Litter training tips:

Use a different kind of litter (such as paper pellets) in the box than in the rest of the cage, and place a small plastic box or tray in a chosen bathroom area of the cage.
 To teach them where to go, move some dirty bedding or droppings into the litter box.
 When they use the box appropriately, give them biscuits as a reward.

The majority of rats will eventually start using the box often, particularly for urinating, which will simplify cleaning and lessen cage smells.

Handling Aggression or Shyness:

Some fancy rats may display shyness, fear, or aggression as a result of prior trauma, improper handling, or health problems, but the majority are kind, gregarious, and ready for company.

Shy Rats:

Rats that are timid or shy may hide, freeze, or stay away from people.

How to assist them:

Take your time and give them room.
Speak in gentle, comforting tones.
Present sweets without first touching them.
Slowly create connections that are beneficial.
Allow interactions to occur to you; never try to force them.

Many timid rats eventually become very loving friends.

Rats that are aggressive:

Although uncommon, true aggressiveness may occur, particularly in male rats who have not been neutered or in rats that have hormonal or dominance-related problems.

Aggression warning signs:

Excessive dominance over cagemates   Fluffed fur, side-shuffling, or boxing posture   Lunging, biting without provocation

Aggression-reduction measures:

Have a veterinarian check to rule out discomfort or sickness.
If hormones play a role, think about spaying or neutering.
Experiment with introducing rats to neutral regions.
If required, put on protective gloves for early handling.
Set strong but calm limits rather than resorting to punishment.

Extreme aggressiveness may need expert assistance from an exotic veterinarian or seasoned rat handler.

Conclusion:

The goal of socialization and training is to build a strong, reciprocal link between you and your rats, not only to make them simpler to manage. The time you spend engaging with your rats will pay you in the form of trust, love, and happiness, from taming timid animals to teaching them tricks and potty routines. Emotional and clever, fancy rats thrive on interaction, affection, and attention. Whether you're caring for a fearful rescue or dealing with an inquisitive new infant, your kindness and patience may change both of your lives.

CHAPTER 9: OPTIONAL REPRODUCTION AND BREEDING

Given how cute young rats, sometimes known as "pups," are, some pet owners may find the thought of breeding elegant rats to be an alluring one. Rat reproduction, however, is a delicate and complicated subject that has to be handled with awareness, accountability, and a strong sense of morality. This chapter examines the reasons why breeding should only be done carefully, the workings of rat reproduction, what to anticipate during pregnancy and delivery, and the critical role that population management and moral behavior play in rat society.

Reasons Why Breeding Must Be Done Only Carefully:

Breeding rats is not a hobby, even if the idea of having a litter of newborn rats may seem endearing. For the animals involved, there are genuine dangers, obligations, and long-term repercussions. Careless breeding may result in:

Overcrowding, poor health outcomes, a rise in shelter euthanasia, genetic abnormalities, and shorter progeny lifespans.

Conscious breeders put their rats' welfare first. They avoid breeding for looks alone, assess the health of their breeding animals, keep stringent genetic records, and make sure each pup is placed in a proper, loving home. Rats bred carelessly or in backyards, on the other hand, often have behavioral issues, physical abnormalities, or a propensity for major illnesses such tumors or respiratory disorders.

Breaking should be avoided unless you are skilled and totally dedicated to the welfare of both parents and offspring. Adopting rather than breeding promotes ethical care since there are always rats in rescues that need homes.

Comprehending the Reproductive Behavior of Rats:

It is common for fancy rats to breed. A couple of rats may have hundreds of offspring in a year if they are not closely watched.

Fundamental Reproductive Information:

Sexual maturity: Although reputable breeders seldom breed female rats younger than 12–16 weeks, rats reach sexual maturity between 4 and 6 weeks of age.
Gestation: around three weeks, or 21–23 days.
Litter size: Usually, a litter has 6–12 puppies, but sometimes there are more than 15.
Heat cycles: Female rats may conceive again within hours after giving birth and enter estrus every 4-5 days.

Lifespan impact: Recurrent pregnancies reduce a woman's life expectancy and raise her chance of problems such as exhaustion, uterine infections, and dystocia (difficult delivery).

Rats don't live together. When the female is in estrus, a short encounter known as mating begins. She will let the man mount by arching her back. Males often engage in pre-courtship rituals including sniffing and grooming.

In order to avoid unwanted pregnancies:

Unless you are actively and morally reproducing, keep men and females apart at all times.
When adopting or purchasing young rats, be sure to thoroughly check the sexes since misidentification is a typical error.

Being pregnant, giving birth, and caring for puppies:

It's important to know how to care for the mother rat and her young if breeding does take place, whether on purpose or by accident.

Indications of pregnancy:

Nest-building activities, Increased hunger and exhaustion, Slight stomach, swelling around the end of the second week, Enlargement of the breasts.

Use soft, odorless nesting materials, such as shredded paper, to create a calm, stress-free environment for the expectant mother. In the latter days of pregnancy, try not to handle her too much.

Date of Birth:

Typically, the woman gives birth in the middle of the night or early in the morning. Usually, labor takes one to two hours. It is usual and healthy for her to clean the puppies right away and consume the placenta.

She may reject or hurt the puppies if she is under stress, so don't bother her while she is in labor.

Taking Care of Pups:

Newborn rats have no hair, are blind, and are deaf. They have to remain warm and breastfeed all the time. They start consuming solid food at three weeks, develop fur between days seven and ten, and open their eyes around day fourteen. By four to five weeks, they are weaned.

In this period:

Don't separate puppies unless it's really necessary. Make sure the mother has clean water and extra food.

After 10–14 days, start handling gently to encourage sociability.

To avoid back-breeding, males must be kept apart from their mother and sisters for 5 weeks.

Population control and ethical considerations:

Animal suffering is a result of careless rat breeding. Beyond providing physical care, ethical issues include considering the lives that are being brought into the world in the long run.

Important Moral Questions to Consider Before Breeding:

Am I enhancing the breed's lifespan, health, and temperament in addition to its looks?
Do I have homes with individuals who know how to take care of rats lined up for each pup?
Can I pay for the mother's and the infants' veterinarian treatment in the event of problems?
Do I have enough time to care for, interact with, and keep an eye on each infant for six to eight weeks?
Do I have enough room to keep unadopted puppies, particularly if they don't find homes?

It's recommended to avoid breeding if any of these answers are "no."

Alternatives for Population Control:

Spaying/neutering: Some exotic veterinarians offer this procedure, particularly for aggressive or hormonally driven males, however it is seldom performed on rats owing to their tiny size and anesthetic risks.
Accurately sexing young rats: Acquire the ability to distinguish between male and female rats at a young age.
Adopt, don't breed: Because of unintentional litters, many rats are turned over to shelters and rescues. Adoption lessens the strain on rescuers and saves lives.

Conclusion:

Fancy rat breeding is a serious endeavor that should never be treated lightly. Although giving birth and rearing puppies may be an exciting and lovely experience, there are hazards and obligations involved. Each life of a fancy rat demands careful attention from start to finish since they are clever, loving animals. Breeding should only be done for the correct reasons, such as maintaining good genetics, enhancing temperament, and making sure each child is desired and well-cared for.

The best course of action for the majority of pet rat owners is to prioritize appropriate companionship, enrichment, and adopting from ethical breeders or rescues. This promotes the general wellbeing of rats worldwide in addition to keeping your rats content and healthy.

CHAPTER 10: PLAYTIME AND ENRICHMENT

For a fancy rat to be healthy and happy overall, playing and enrichment are crucial. Rats need much more than simply food, drink, and shelter to survive since they are very gregarious and clever creatures. Their emotional and cognitive health depends on mental stimulation, exercise, and meaningful connection with people and other rats. A bored rat is more prone to depression, destructive behavior, and health issues. The significance of mental stimulation, different enrichment techniques including do-it-yourself toys and foraging games, how to create secure play spaces outside of cages, and how to encourage social play between rats and people will all be covered in this chapter.

The Value of Mental Exercise

Rats are among the smartest small pets; they are sometimes likened to dogs and even certain primates in terms of their capacity for learning. Rats in the wild are continuously engaged by interacting with people, exploring, foraging, and negotiating challenging surroundings. Without enough stimulation, they may get bored, irritated, and even unhappy while in captivity. Pet rats' mental stimulation improves:

Cognitive health: Rats that solve puzzles or make their way through mazes maintain mental acuity.
Emotional health: Rats that are allowed to engage in natural activities like climbing, foraging, and digging are less likely to experience anxiety and are more self-assured.
Behavioral balance: Stress-related behaviors such as aggressiveness, excessive grooming, and cage biting are less common in stimulated rats.
Longevity: Because they are more active and experience less stress, mentally enhanced rats often have longer, healthier lives.

Rats who get mental stimulation are happier, and happier rats have more satisfying lives and greater relationships with their owners.

DIY Games and Toys for Foraging

To make your rats' life better, you don't need to invest a lot of money. Safe, everyday household materials may be used to create some of the most successful games and toys at home.

Have Your Own Toys:

1. Cardboard Tunnels and Mazes: Construct labyrinths, tunnels, and hiding places out of cardboard boxes and paper towel rolls. Verify that the supplies are free of adhesive and clean.

2. Egg Carton Puzzles: Stuff a treat-filled egg carton, seal it, and let your rats discover a way to extract the food.

3. Hanging Chew Mobiles: Attach little bells, cardboard, and wooden blocks to string and suspend them from the cage's top.

4. Shredding Fun: Offer napkins, paper towels, or crumpled paper for nesting and shredding.

5. Digging Box: Bury goodies in a small box filled with sand, clean, odorless dirt, or torn paper. This fulfills innate desires for foraging and digging.

6. PVC Pipes: Tunnels and obstacle courses are ideal for non-toxic plumbing pipes.

7. Climbing Ladders and Ropes: To provide climbing chances both inside and outside the cage, use hammocks, wooden ladders, or sisal rope.

8. Snack Kebabs: Attach fruits or vegetables on a kabob stick or stainless steel rod, then hang them in the cage for rats to munch on.

When giving your rats new toys, always keep an eye on them to make sure there are no sharp edges or bits they may ingest. Every few days, switch up the toys to make the space interesting and new.

Games of Foraging:

Rats spend a great deal of time looking for food in the wild. With entertaining foraging activities that test their cognitive abilities and satisfy their curiosity, you may simulate this impulse.

Game Ideas for Foraging:

Using paper or tissue, wrap little items into "candy" shapes by twisting the ends. Unwrapping it will be fun for your rats.

Scavenger Hunts: Place food scraps in a play area or around their cage and let them locate them.

Treat Cups: Fill little paper cups with snacks, then cover them with other cups. Rats may dig into them or topple them over.

Puzzle Feeders: To make treat-hunting more difficult, use puzzle toys made for little dogs or even adapted dog puzzle toys.

Frozen Treat Balls: Fill tiny molds with water or sugar-free yogurt, then mix with acceptable fruit or peas. In order to get the sweets, rats like to lick and chew.

Foraging keeps rats interested and promotes natural problem-solving, particularly when you're not around to engage them.

Safe Play Spaces Outside of Cages:

A rat's physical and mental demands cannot be satisfied by cage living, no matter how well-equipped it is. Playtime outside of cages must be regular and supervised.

Ideal Playtime Length and Frequency:

At least 1 hour each day, preferably divided into two or more sessions. Playing well for even 30 minutes may have a significant impact on one's health and emotions.

Creating a Secure Play Space:

Rattery-proof the area Rats are inquisitive and will gnaw on furniture, wiring, and other hazardous materials. To keep children contained, use playpens or obstacles.

Exploration under supervision: Never let rats alone outside of their cage. They can swiftly gnaw through objects or fit into small areas.

Comfort and familiarity: To make rats feel safe, provide hammocks, hiding boxes, or familiar toys in the play area.

Vertical space: To promote physical activity, include climbing options such as boxes, ramps, or ropes.

Soft landings: To avoid fall injuries, make sure there is soft bedding or mats underneath any raised platforms.

Some excellent choices for play spaces are:

A large playpen with high, chew-resistant walls, A bed or sofa that is blanketed and encircled by barriers, and a restroom that has been rat-proofed.

To establish a good connection, gently put your rats back in their cage after playing, maybe even with a tiny reward.

Interaction with Humans and Other Rats:

Rats are gregarious creatures that inherently seek for company, both from their human caregivers and from other rats.

Play between Rats:

Rats are always playing with one another. They still wrestle, chase, and groom even as adults. These actions foster connection and are normal.

Wrestling: It's common to wrestle gently and playfully. It's typically harmless fun as long as there isn't any blood, excessive shrieking, or biting.

Mutual grooming: When rats groom one another, they are demonstrating love and trust.

Sleeping in piles: Rats often sleep curled up together because they find comfort in physical proximity.

Always use the gradual introduction method to introduce new rats gradually and on neutral ground to promote safe, contented relationships.

Human-Rat Communication:

Playing with rats fosters trust and deep emotional bonds between humans and rats. Here are a few entertaining ways to interact with your rats:

Pursue the hand: Move your fingers about the floor; a lot of rats will gleefully jump and pursue.

Peekaboo: Sneak out from behind items. Rats often think this is funny and will look into it.

Tug toys: A simple tug-of-war game may be played using a knotted rope or a strip of fabric.

Training sessions: Play and mental stimulation are combined when tricks are taught via positive reinforcement.

Lap time and cuddles: Although not all rats are cute, many of them like to perch on your shoulder, hide in your clothing, or just relax on your lap.

Additionally, social play strengthens relationships, fosters trust, and eventually facilitates handling and care.

Conclusion:

Play and enrichment are essential to the health of any pet rat, not extravagance. Intelligent, active, and gregarious, fancy rats thrive in situations that are stimulating, their intellect are active, and their social requirements are satisfied. Every chance to engage your rats' senses enhances their happiness and quality of life, from safe out-of-cage excursions and affectionate social interactions to foraging activities and do-it-yourself toys.

Putting effort and imagination into your rats' daily routines not only increases their happiness but also fortifies the special link you have with your little friends. The cornerstone of responsible, caring rat ownership is a well-enriched rat, which is not only physically fit but also emotionally content.

CHAPTER 11: TRAVELING AND BOARDING

A difficult but doable aspect of pet ownership is taking your fancy rats on trips or making arrangements for their care while you're gone. Careful preparation is essential to reducing stress and danger, whether it's a long-term relocation, a quick holiday, or a trip to the veterinarian. Since fancy rats are delicate animals that rely significantly on stability and security, it is crucial to move them securely, recruit qualified caretakers, and provide appropriate temporary homes. This chapter will go over how to properly move rats, set up temporary housing, prepare a travel carrier, and find boarding facilities or pet sitters that have expertise with rats.

Safe Rat Transportation:

There is more to transporting rats than just putting them in a box or little cage. To guarantee their comfort, safety, and health, extra care must be given since they are little, delicate, and quickly stressed.

Contexts in Which Transportation Is Required:

Regular veterinary checkups; emergency medical attention; relocating or home shifting; hiring a pet sitter; and vacation or long-distance travel

Overall Advice for Secure Transportation:

1. Select a suitable carrier: A safe, well-ventilated travel carrier is essential (see below for additional details).
2. **Reduce stress:** Reduce noise, vibrations, and abrupt motions.

3. Rats are very sensitive to heat and cold, so stay away from extremely hot or cold conditions. The ideal temperature range for travel is 18–24°C (65–75°F).

4. Only groups connected rats together; avoid overcrowding. Do not overburden one carrier.

5. **Keep travels short**: Try to keep travel time to a minimum. Long trips might make people more anxious and raise their risk of dehydration or hyperthermia.

6. **Observe conduct**: Lethargy, hiding, excessive grooming, and panting are all indicators of stress. Provide comfort and make necessary adjustments.

Crucial: A rat carrier should never be kept in the trunk of a car or in direct sunlight. Throughout the journey, they need a steady habitat and access to fresh air.

Getting a Carrier Ready:

The secret to a successful and safe vacation is using the right travel agency. During transportation, your rats should be safe, cozy, and shielded from outside threats.

The Qualities of an Effective Carrier:

The rats are just big enough to lay down, turn around, and move a little. They could be jostled during transit if they are too big.

Material: Secure fabric carriers or hard plastic work well. Rats can gnaw through cardboard, so stay away from it.

Ventilation: Make sure there is enough airflow, but stay away from wide openings that might cause escapes or drafts.

Simple to maintain: It may be untidy to travel, particularly on longer excursions. Select a carrier with a base that can be removed or cleaned.

Safe door: The latch has to be impenetrable. Surprisingly, rats can force weak closures open.

Checklist for Carrier Preparation:

1. **Bedding:** Make use of cozy, comfortable bedding (such as paper or fleece). Steer clear of loose items that might spread while being transported.
2. **Hiding spot**: To make the rats feel safe, provide a little hiding place, such as a tissue box or pouch.
3. **Absorbent layer:** To collect spills or pee, use a towel or puppy pad on the foundation.
Eating and drinking water:

During brief excursions, provide high-moisture items like apple slices or cucumber to keep them hydrated. Attach a water bottle with a no-leak spout for trips longer than two hours, but be sure to check often to prevent leaks.
5. **Confidence objects or treats**: To ease nervousness, place a cherished toy or a homey scent.

To stop the carrier from moving while traveling by automobile, fasten it with a seatbelt. The carrier may slide or fall during abrupt stops, so never carry it on your lap.

Transient Accommodation Configurations:

Your rats will need a temporary home that offers security, comfort, and basic conveniences if you want to spend the night elsewhere or move temporarily.

Uses for Short-Term Housing:

A small, multi-level cage is ideal, preferably one that your rats are used to.

Collapsible playpens: Not the best option for unsupervised housing, but excellent for supervised free time.

Travel cages: For short-term usage (up to a few days), small cages with solid bottoms and bar spacing under 1/2 inch are appropriate.

Bin cages: Although they must be escape-proof and well-ventilated, large plastic containers with improved ventilation may be temporarily effective, particularly during relocation.

Important Things for Short-Term Accommodations:

1. Bedding To make the transfer easier, use the same bedding as in their primary cage.
2. **Hides**: Set up areas for hiding, including cardboard boxes, hammocks, or igloos.
3. **Food and water**: Make sure that a water bottle or dish and familiar food are always available.
4. **Toys:** Provide simple enrichment such as ropes, tunnels, or chew toys.
5. **Cleaning supplies**: To keep things hygienic, include cage wipes, additional bedding, and bags for disposing of waste.

Transition Tip: To lessen stress, attempt to replicate certain aspects of your rats' typical surroundings if they will be in temporary housing for more than a day or two. Make use of hammocks, toys, and familiar scents.

Looking for Pet Sitters with Rat Experience:

It becomes important to leave your rats in the care of someone else if you are unable to take them with you. But not all boarding houses or pet sitters are prepared to deal with rats in a safe manner. Compared to dogs, cats, or even other tiny animals, fancy rats need a very different kind of care.

The Significance of Experience:

Rats need regular social engagement and mental stimulation, and they have special nutritional, medical, and environmental requirements. Ignorance or poor management might result in sickness, injury, or escape.

How to Locate a Fit Sitter:

1. **Word of mouth:** Consult breeders, Facebook groups, online rat forums, or your neighborhood rat community.
2. **Recommendations from veterinarians:** Exotic veterinarians often know sitters who have experience with rats.
3. **Pet sitting networks:** You may search by species cared for on websites such as Rover or TrustedHousesitters; always confirm experience.
4. **Animal rescues:** Some small animal rescues have volunteers who can assist or give short-term boarding.

Qualities to Consider in a Boarding or Sitting Service:

Possessing a clean, safe, and escape-proof habitat; being able to handle and house rats; being willing to follow directions exactly; having access to an exotic veterinarian in case of problems; and having experience giving medicine (if necessary)

Getting Ready to Be Away:

Provide emergency contact information, including your veterinarian's number; Include comprehensive written directions for feeding, cleaning, playing, and any health issues.

For the duration of your visit, bring adequate food, snacks, blankets, and toys.

Make sure you accurately label all prescriptions and supplies.

If at all feasible, do a trial run to aid your rats in becoming used to the sitter.

The best course of action if your rats need specialist care or have a complicated medical issue is to have a veterinary technician or rat-savvy caretaker.

Conclusion:

Both rats and their caretakers may find travel and boarding unpleasant, but these situations may be handled securely and amicably with the correct preparation and tools. The most important thing is to put your pets' comfort, safety, and familiarity first, whether you're moving, taking your rodents to the doctor, or leaving them with someone else while you're gone. You can make sure that your fancy rats are safe, healthy, and emotionally stable even when you're not around by using the right travel carriers, keeping temporary settings clean and consistent, and choosing a reliable sitter with rat-specific knowledge.

In addition to making travel easier, careful planning builds trust between you and your rats. After all, a well-maintained rat is more than just a pet; they are a cherished friend that deserves the greatest treatment possible, regardless of the situation.

CHAPTER 12: SAYING FAREWELL AND THE HUMAN-RAT BOND

A special and very fulfilling experience, owning fancy rats is characterized by love, trust, and camaraderie. Rats may develop strong emotional bonds with their human caretakers despite their little stature. They are very gregarious, clever, and expressive, and they often win as many affections as any dog or cat. However, the pleasure of living with rats is accompanied with a significant emotional cost: rats have a very short existence. One of the most difficult aspects of rat ownership is adjusting to their age, sickness, and ultimate loss.

The emotional aspects of living with and eventually bidding farewell to your rat pals are examined in this last chapter. It talks about how strong the human-rat link is, how short their lives are, how to help them deal with old age and disease, and how to deal with the loss that comes when they die.

The Emotional Aspect of Rat Ownership;

Before seeing it firsthand, many people underestimate the emotional depth of a rat-human interaction. More than just pets, fancy rats are partners with unique personalities, tastes, and methods of expressing love.

The Relationship You Form:

A remarkable friendship may develop as soon as a rat starts to trust you. They know your routine, your voice, and your fragrance. They anxiously await you at the cage entrance after learning your schedule. They cuddle in your sweater, ride on your shoulder, and softly rub your face or fingers. They want to be with you and get your attention. Rats are very clever animals that react loyally and affectionately to kindness.

The more time passes, the deeper this friendship gets. As a result of your understanding of their nuanced actions, they feel more secure with you. Losing a rat is often quite distressing because of that fundamental trust.

Aware of Their Limited Lifespan?

Even under ideal conditions, rats have tragically short lives, which is one of the worst realities of rat ownership. Even with perfect care, very few luxury rats survive until their third birthday, and their typical lifetime is just 2 to 3 years.

The Reasons Behind Their Brief Lives:

Like other rodents, rats age quickly due to their fast metabolisms, and common health issues like tumors or respiratory infections may drastically reduce their lifespan. Lifespan is also significantly influenced by genetics.

Rats mature so rapidly that they may go from inquisitive young animals to respectable elderly people in an instant. You could see them slowing down or showing indications of fragility shortly after they start zoomies and scaling the cage bars.

Emotional Implications of This:

When you own rats, you have to accept the bittersweet fact that you will probably outlast them all. Loving deeply while realizing that time is limited is a difficult but worthwhile path. And the love and gratitude you experience each day they are with you may be strengthened by this very knowing.

Managing Euthanasia, Aging, and Illness:

You will eventually have to take care of your rat when their health deteriorates, just as you would with any other cherished pet. You take on the roles of consoler, protector, and decision-maker as a result of age, disease, or injury.

Indications of Rat Aging:

Loss of weight and muscle mass Weakness in the hind legs (degeneration of the hind limbs) Less activity or more sleep Dental problems or trouble eating Scabs, thinning hair, or respiratory symptoms.

More regular veterinarian care, ramps rather than shelves, softer bedding, and better access to food and water are all necessary for older rats. In their last months, they also want company and comfort, warmth, kind words, and hugs are more important than ever.

Typical End-of-Life Health Issues:

Respiratory illness: Chronic infections may become incurable Kidney failure or organ degeneration.
Neurological issues: disorientation, seizures, or lack of coordination.
Tumors: especially breast tumors, which may be benign or malignant.

As their body deteriorates, pain management, nourishment, and cleanliness become your main considerations.

The Euthanasia Decision:

The choice of whether to put a suffering rat to sleep is the most agonizing one a rat owner may have to make. The choice was made out of love, not weakness. Euthanasia could be the greatest humane present you can give a rat who is in excruciating agony, unable to feed, or no longer interested in life.

A exotic veterinarian may assist you in determining quality of life, so work closely with them. Usually consisting of a sedative and a painless injection, the procedure is short and quiet.

Being there when your rat is put to sleep may be very challenging, but it can also be consoling. They will be the last to remember your voice, your touch, and your perfume. Being there is an act of dedication and affection.

Respecting the Memory of Your Rat:

A rat's death causes genuine and legitimate sadness. Your loss is not insignificant just because they are little creatures. A friend, family member, or partner who knew you in a way that few others could have passed away.

Meths to Honor and Remember Them:

1. Make a Memory Box: Save a paw print, some of their toys, or pictures.
2. Write a Tribute: Write a letter to them or write in your journal about your best recollections.
3. Conduct a Ceremony: A simple burial or ash dispersal might provide closure.
4. Plant a Tree or Flower: Honor them by symbolizing life going on.
Create Art: A lot of rats' owners paint, sketch, or commission artwork of their pets.

Managing Bereavement:

Everybody grieves in a unique way. Before letting another rat into their house, some people require some time. Others take solace in continuing to tend to the surviving rats. There isn't a proper or improper method to grieve.

Discuss your loss with sympathetic friends, particularly other rat lovers. Pet grief support groups and internet forums might be helpful. Additionally, don't be scared to weep. Your suffering is a reflection of the love you offered, and that love was very important.

A Concluding Remark: The Present of Adoring a Rat;

We can learn a lot from fancy rats. They teach us the importance of being present in the moment, the beauty of company, and the thrill of freely offered trust. During their brief stay with us, they offer all they have and want very little in return.

Despite their brief existence, they make a lasting impression. You will alter with every rat you love. They will teach you to be patient, polite, and to value the time you have left. And you will always have them in your heart once they are gone.

It takes bravery to choose to love something with such a limited lifespan. And it is an act of grace to decide to stay to the very end.

Printed in Dunstable, United Kingdom